D1306292

KHAJURAHO
ORCHHA

KHAJURAHO
ORCHHA

Text:

ARCHANA SHANKAR

Lustre Press
·
Roli Books

© **Roli & Janssen BV 1997**

All rights reserved. No part of this publication
may be reproduced or transmitted in any
form or by any means without prior
permission of the publisher.

ISBN: 81-7437-087-0

Fifth impression 2003
Published in India by
Roli Books in arrangement
with Roli & Janssen BV
M-75, Greater Kailash II Market
New Delhi-110 048, India
Ph: ++91 (11) 29210886, 29212782
Fax: ++91 (11) 29217185
E-mail: roli@vsnl.com; Website: rolibooks.com

Text Editor
Bela Butalia

Production
Naresh Nigam, Abhijit Raha

Typesetting
Naresh L. Mondal

Concept & Design
Roli CAD Centre

Photo Credits

Sondeep Shankar
Dheeraj Paul
Pramod Kapoor
Lustre Press Library

Printed and bound in Singapore

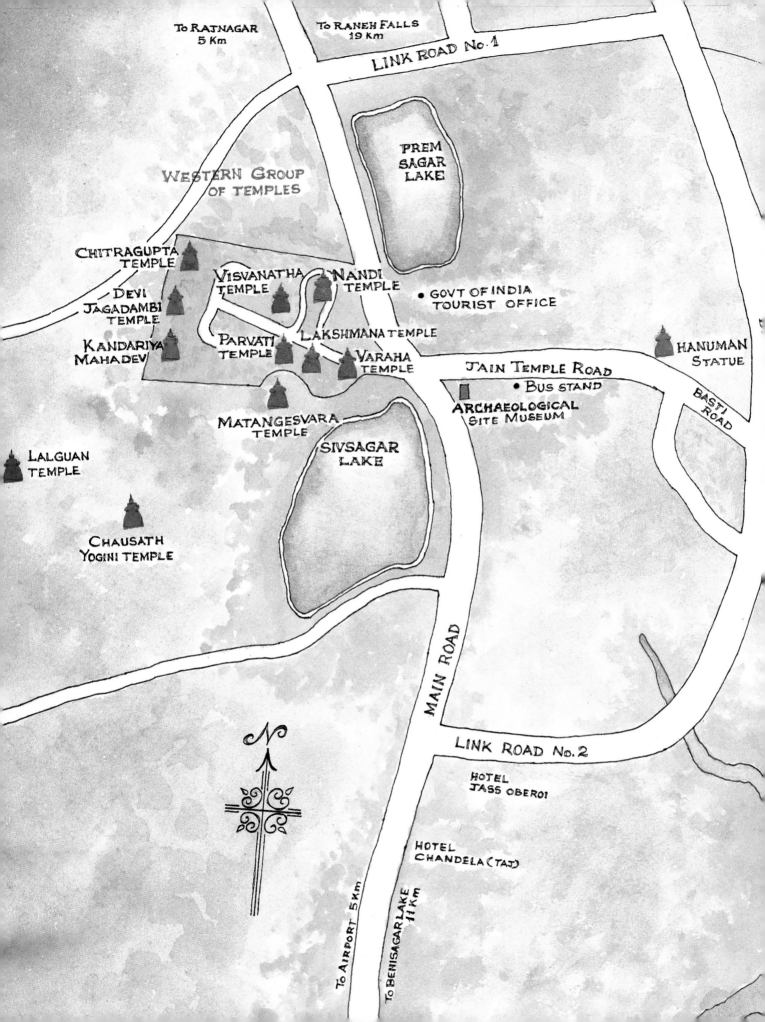

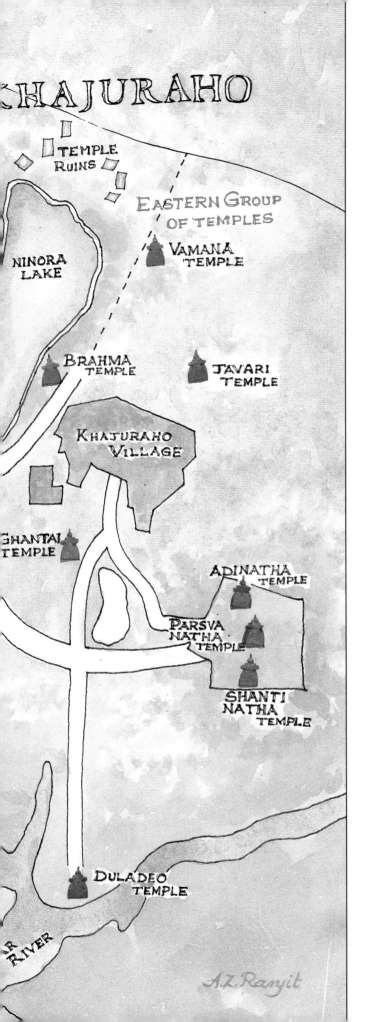

KHAJURAHO

TEMPLE RUINS

EASTERN GROUP OF TEMPLES

VAMANA TEMPLE

NINORA LAKE

BRAHMA TEMPLE

JAVARI TEMPLE

KHAJURAHO VILLAGE

GHANTAI TEMPLE

ADINATHA TEMPLE

PARSVA NATHA TEMPLE

SHANTI NATHA TEMPLE

DULADEO TEMPLE

RIVER

A.Z.Ranjit

*O*ne thousand years ago, 85 extraordinary temples were constructed near Khajuraho under the patronage of the Chandella kings who ruled over the area from the 9th to the 14th century. The remains of only 25 of these temples survive, extending over an area of 21 sq. km. around the village and constitute one of the most alluring temple sites in India. The erotic sculptures, the subject of numerous interpretations, are the best known but these form only a small part of the total wealth of the site. Built in a burst of creative energy, the temples, a joyous celebration of life, are among the artistic wonders of the world. Since their rediscovery in 1838, innumerable travellers, scholars and artists have made Khajuraho a destination.

Preceding page 1: A sculpture of Ganesha outside Matangeshvara temple, the only temple in Khajuraho where there is active worship. According to the Puranas, Ganesha, represented as short, pot-bellied and elephant-headed, is the son of Shiva and Parvati . He is venerated as the remover of obstacles and is invoked at the beginning of any new venture.

Pages 8-9: A visitor's first view upon entering the western group of temples.

Pages 10-11: The south-facing facade of the Parsvanatha temple, the largest local Jaina temple. Three rows of panels of decreasing size are set in shallow recesses and projections. The topmost band carries figures of flying *vidyadharas* and attendants carying garlands and musical instruments. The other bands are embellished with sculptures of divinities with or without their consorts. Mythical beasts are set in the recesses, leaving no voids.

Pages 12-13: A panel from the lowest of three bands on the facade of the Parsvanatha temple. The *apsara* applying collyrium is a sculpture common to the western group as well. *Shardulas* flank the *apsara* on both sides. On her left is the traditional horse-lion combination. On her right is the more unusual elephant-lion *shardula*. These in turn are flanked by images of Balram (Lord Krishna's older brother) and his consort Revati on the left, and by Vishnu and his consort Lakshmi on the right.

Pages 14-15: One of a series of erotic panels in the Kandariya Mahadeva temple. Several explanations have been offered for the existence of erotic panels in a place of worship. It was variously speculated that they were an interpretation of the *Kama Sutra* or a Tantric rite which gave sexual intercourse a ceremonial significance.

Following pages 18-19: The diffused light that enters the sanctum gently illuminates the surrounding panels of sculpture.
Pages20-21: Depictions of coupled figures on a running frieze on an outer panel, Lakshmana temple.
Pages 22-23: Orchha, 160 km from Khajuraho. Now little more than a village, it was the capital of the Bundela Rajputs during the 16th and 17th centuries; they built a small city, citadel, palaces and *chhatris*.

Surasundaris or celestial beauties, Devi Jagdambi temple. The female figures that embellish the temples at Khajuraho are elegant and typically twist around the axis in the *tribhanga* pose, evoking a languid and sensual air.

Matangeshvara Temple, dedicated to Shiva
Built in *c*. AD 900-925 during the reign of Harshadeva.

Lakshmana Temple, dedicated to Vishnu
Built in *c*. AD 930-950 during the reign of Yasovarman.

Varaha Temple, dedicated to Vishnu
Built in *c*. AD 900-925 during the reign of Harshadeva.

Kandariya Mahadeva Temple, dedicated to Shiva
Built in *c*. AD 1025-50 during the reigns of Vidyadhara
(*c*. 1017-1029) and Vijaipal (*c*. 1029-1051).

Devi Jagdambi Temple, dedicated to Parvati.
Originally dedicated to Vishnu.
Built in *c*. AD 1000 during the latter part of
Dhangadeva's reign (*c*. 954-1002).

Vishvanatha Temple, dedicated to Shiva
Built in AD 1002 by Dhangadeva.

Adinatha Temple, dedicated to Adinath,
the first Jain *Tirthankara*.
Built in the late 11th century during the
reign of Kirtivarman.

Parsvanatha Temple, dedicated to Adinatha
Built in *c*. AD 954 during the early part of
Dhangadeva's reign.

Vamana Temple, dedicated to Vishnu
Built in *c*. AD 1050-1075 during the
reign of Salakshanvarman.

Brahma Temple, dedicated to Vishnu
Built in *c*. AD 900.

Duladeo Temple, dedicated to Shiva
Built in *c*. AD 1100-1125.

Chaturbhuj Temple, dedicated to Shiva
Built in *c*. AD 1100.

Through the Veils of History

*K*hajuraho would have been like any small central Indian village but for its legacy of a group of extraordinary temples which pushed it to the forefront of worldwide attention. Under the patronage of the later Chandella kings who ruled over the area from the 9th to the 14th centuries, a distinctive school of architecture flourished which was manifested in these temples. The remains of the ancient temples of Khajuraho extend over an area of twenty-one square kilometres around the village and are today among the most captivating temple sites in India. Eighty-five temples are believed to have been built—twenty-five still stand in varying states of preservation—over a period of a little over two centuries, and mark the culmination of the north Indian Nagara (Indo-Aryan) style of temple architecture. Some of the finest sculptural compositions, which are among the masterpieces of Indian art, adorn these temples. Integrated with the architecture are forms of divinities, semi-divine figures, *dikpalas* (guardians of the cardinal directions), *apsaras* (celestial dancers) and *surasundaris* (celestial beauties), *vidyadharas* (angels), *gandharvas* (celestial musicians), *ganas* (cherubs) and *maithunas* (amorous couples) which are juxtaposed with decorative and symbolic floral or geometric patterns set in deep recesses, making for an interplay of elaborately carved sculptures and mellow shadows. Continuous narrative friezes, depicting music and dance, court life, battle, processions, rituals, ceremonies, domestic life and couples loving or in repose, run along bands inside and outside the temples in a joyous celebration of the human form and the whole gamut of its activity. Although the erotic sculptures are the

A frieze from the Lakshmana temple. The lowest tier depicts a procession of musicians; the middle tier a battle scene; the topmost tier shows ascetics with women.

27

best known, they form less than one-tenth of the sculptures. The figures, apparently poised in movement, are warm, graceful, languid and sensuous, redolent of a feeling of unity with nature and a sense of well-being. Real and mythical animals are also a ubiquitous motif.

For many centuries, Khajuraho remained a little-known village, concealed by dense jungles. In 1838, when a British army engineer Captain T. S. Burt chanced upon Khajuraho, it appeared to have been abandoned for over seven hundred years. Its inaccessibility saved it from Muslim destruction. When the area was surveyed in 1818, Khajuraho was written off as ruins. Since the rediscovery of the temples, the village, which is miles from the nearest town, has been visited by innumerable travellers, scholars and artists. Daily flights connect Khajuraho with Delhi, Agra and Varanasi. The nearest railway stations are Satna (117 km) and Jhansi (175 km).

The present-day village of Khajuraho is situated in the district of Chhatarpur in Madhya Pradesh, central India. The country around Khajuraho is well-watered by the Narmada and Chambal, and cradled among hillocks, offshoots of the Panna range which belong to the Vindhya mountains, a natural line of demarcation between north and south India and one of its seven principal mountain chains. Twenty kilometres east of the village is the river Ken, which rises in the Vindhyas and flows in a northeasterly direction till it meets the Jamuna, a major tributary of the river Ganga. The quarries of Panna, on the east bank of the Ken, provided the hard, fine-grained, pink, pale buff and yellow sandstone, called Kaimur which was used to great advantage by Khajuraho's artists.

The climate is tropical and the land, which is upland, appears flat and is segmented into basins; in ancient times rain water was gathered in tanks and bunds—it is believed there were sixty—of which there are visible remains. Now there are no more than three large tanks: Khajurasagar, Shiv Sagar and Prem Sagar, used for ceremonial and domestic purposes. The village—with a population of about 8,000, most

A column from the Ghantai Temple. The temple gets its name from the chain-and-bell *(ghantai)* motifs.

of which lives in mud-houses with clay-tile roofs—is now clustered around Khajurasagar, also known as Ninoratal, and is spread over an area that hardly exceeds eight square kilometres. The terrain, dotted with mahua trees whose flowers are used to brew the local liquor, permits intermittent cultivation.

The name Khajuraho is derived from *khajura* (date palm) which grew in abundance in the area. Legend has it that Khajuraho's ancient city gates were ornamented with two carved golden *khajura* trees after which it was named. The tract around Khajuraho was known during ancient times, until 400 BC, as Vatsa, in medieval times as Jejabhukti (with a few variants like Jejahauti, Jajhauti and Jijhauti), and since the fourteenth century as Bundelkhand. The Chandellas, who became prominent in the ninth century and ruled over Jejabhukti, were a Rajput tribe who claimed descent from the moon through the legendary sage Chandratreya. The *Prithviraja-raso*, an epic poem by Chand Bardai, a medieval Indian poet in the court of Prithviraj Chauhan III (1177-92), ruler of Delhi and Ajmer, tells of the young daughter of a Brahmin priest, Hemavati, who was seduced by the moon god, Chandra, while she was bathing in a lotus pond, Rati Talab, in Kashi (Varanasi). The moon god advised Hemavati to go to Khajuraho where their son would be born and would grow up to become a great king. Hemavati left her home in Kashi and reached Khajuraho where, in due course, Chandravarman, the progenitor of the Chandellas, was born. Chandravarman did indeed become a dauntless hero; by the time he was sixteen years old, he could slay a lion bare-handed. The emblem of the Chandellas became a young man grappling with a lion, a scene on which there are several sculptures at Khajuraho.

According to a variation of this story, which also ascribes to Chandratreya the dynasty of the Chandellas, Hemavati was the daughter of Mani Ram, a priest of the ruler of Kalanjar, eighty kilometres from Khajuraho. On a particular moonless night, miscalculating the movement of the planets, Mani Ram informed the king that there would be a full moon. When the mistake was discovered, Hemavati, to save her father's reputation, prayed to the moon god to appear; he obliged but, captivated by her beauty, also ravished her. Mortified, Mani Ram cursed himself and turned into stone. In due course, Chandratreya, the begetter of the Chandellas, was born. Maniya-deva, whose shrines still exists at Maniyagadh, nineteen kilometres south of Khajuraho, and Mahoba, came to be worshipped as the family deity of the Chandellas.

Historians believe that the Chandellas originated from the aboriginal Gonds. Their domain included Mahoba, fifty-five kilometres

A sculpture of an apsara putting on bell-anklets before a dance performance from the northern facade of the Parsvanatha Temple. The temple bears some of the loveliest images of surasundaris.
Following pages 30-31: A frieze, depicting dancers and musicians, from the plinth of the Lakshmana Temple.

north of Khajuraho, Ajaygarh, Kalanjar and Khajuraho, the last being their capital from the ninth to the twelfth centuries. The forts of Ajaygarh and Kalanjar crowned flat-topped hills, called Dantla (meaning worn-out teeth), which mark the eastern edge of the village. The Chandellas adorned these places, which were their strongholds, as well as Dudhai, Chandpur and Madanpur, which they founded, and Deogarh (to the northwest of Jhansi) with numerous tanks, forts, palaces and Brahmanical and Jain temples, but the splendour of the capital-town of Khajuraho was unrivalled.

The earlier Chandella chiefs were feudatories of the Pratiharas who ruled western and central India after the break up of Harshavardhana's empire in the mid-seventh century. According to various inscriptions, Nannuka was the first sovereign of the dynasty, followed by Vakpati, Jayashakti, and Vijayashakti. At the turn of the tenth century (c. AD 885-905), Vijayashakti's son, Rahila, succeeded him. Rahila is said to have founded the city of Rahilya near Mahoba, identified as a charming site encircled by hills. A Chandella princess, Rahila's sister (or daughter), is believed to have married a ruler from the neighbouring Kalachuri kingdom. Subsequent temples built in Khajuraho demonstrate a marked influence of neighbouring regions; the early Gupta (3rd—5th-century dynasty of central India) temples and those of the Pratiharas (8th to 11th-century rulers of northern and central India who claimed descent from Lakshmana, half-brother of Rama, hero of the epic *Ramayana*) were built during the Chandella era. Artistic and stylistic influences from temples in Osian in Rajasthan, dating from the eighth and ninth centuries, and from Malwa and Orissa in the east are also in evidence in the temples of Khajuraho.

Rahilya was succeeded by his son Harshadeva (c. AD 900-925). Harsha established a large independent kingdom for the Chandellas. It is believed that the Chausath Yogini and the Lalguan Mahadeva, which were the earliest Chandella temples, were built during his reign. His son and successor, the illustrious Yasovarman or Lakshavarman (c. AD 925-950), was even more powerful. He won back from the Rashtrakutas in AD 940, the mountain fort of Kalanjar. The Rashtrakutas had wrested it from the Pratiharas. Warring kings had, for centuries, fought for possession of Kalanjar which was the key to central India and cited in the ancient texts as the "abode of Lord Shiva." The fort houses the Nilkantha *linga* (the phallic symbol of Lord Shiva), an ancient *linga* mentioned in the Puranas (holy scriptures) and still in worship. According to an inscription, Yasovarman built a temple dedicated to Vishnu; it was the most elaborate temple of its time and is now known as the Lakshmana temple. He also built a large tank.

Yasovarman was succeeded by his son Dhanga (c. AD 950-1002). Dhanga consolidated the Chandella kingdom, making it the strongest power in northern India. Under Dhanga, the kingdom included almost all of modern Madhya Pradesh. Dhanga was a great patron of art and architecture. During his reign, two of the finest surviving temples, the Visvanatha and the Parsvanatha, were built. Dhanga's inscriptions at Khajuraho are the source of much of the historical evidence of the Chandella occupation of Khajuraho. An inscription dated AD 954, found among ruins at the Lakshmana temple, is the oldest and establishes that Yasovarman built the temple of Vishnu. Another inscription, dated AD 1002 and found in the Visvanatha temple, records Dhanga's death and also says that he lived for over a hundred years. It refers to Khajur-vahaka, apparently the original form of Khajuraho.

It was, however, the Muslim chroniclers who specifically mention Khajuraho as the capital of the Chandellas. Abu Rihan visited the region in AD 1002 and wrote of Jejabhukti with Kajuraha as its capital.

Dhanga's son and successor was Ganda (c. AD 1002-17) who had a short but peaceful reign. The Vaishnava temple, (now known as Jagadambi), and the Sun temple (known as Chitragupta), are attributed to him.

Ganda was succeeded by his son Vidyadhara (AD 1017-29) who was one of the

The Chausath Yogini temple is the oldest temple at Khajuraho. Made of coarse granite, it is the most primitive in construction of all the *yogini* temples in India and is unique in that it is quadrangular rather than circular in plan.

most powerful rulers of the time. Under him, the Chandella kingdom reached the peak of its prosperity. Besides being a mighty warrior, Vidyadhara also carried forward the great building tradition of his ancestors. The grandest temple in Khajuraho, the 102-foot-high Shaivite Kandariya Mahadeva, has been assigned to his reign. Vidyadhara won victories over the Kalachuris and the Paramaras of Malwa, who were the two rival powers in western India. During his reign, the first Islamic invasions of northwest India were first felt; his grandson, Kirtivarman, referred to it in one of his inscriptions. During Vidyadhara's reign, Mahmud of Ghazni's invasions of Bundelkand were initially contained. Vidyadhara was, however, constrained to accept the nominal suzerainty of the monarch.

After Vidyadhara's death, the political importance of Khajuraho gradually waned. Vidyadhara's successors ruled over Bundelkhand for over a century, but moved to hill-forts elsewhere in their kingdom. Madanavarman (*c.* AD 1129-65), the seventeenth of twenty-two Chandella rulers, defeated the Paramaras, killed the Kalachuri chief and made the Kalachuris his feudatories.

Soon after, the Chandellas were beaten by the Gahadavalas of Kanauj (Varanasi). Madanavarman was succeeded by his grandson, Paramardideva (*c.* AD 1165-1202), who was defeated by Prithviraj Chauhan III in 1182; he lost a large chunk of his territory, including Mahoba, to him. In 1202, Qutubuddin Aibak, the slave general of Mohammed Ghori, invaded Kalanjar; Paramardideva surrendered after a brief struggle, but was put to death by his minister for his cowardice. Subsequently, the Chandella lands came under the grip of the Sultans.

Khajuraho, however, continued to be the religious capital of the Chandellas until the fourteenth century. Ibn Batuta, an Arab

An amorous couple, Devi Jagdambi temple. The expression of intense rapture transcends the physical.

Devi Jagdambi temple. The couple shares a light moment as the woman tugs at the man's necklace.

traveller who visited the area in 1335, describes in his chronicles a place called Kajarra which was inhabited by "jogis with long and clotted hair, their skin yellowed by fasting." He also described "a great pond, about a mile in length, near which are temples containing idols which the Muslims have mutilated." This lake, now known as Khajurasagar, stands 800 metres east of the western group of temples which was probably the heart of the old town.

By the sixteenth century, Khajuraho seems to have lost all importance, turning into an obscure village. It remained lost to the outside world until 1838, when the temples were rediscovered by Captain T. S. Burt. Burt was on official duty, but made a detour from his

Facing page: The Devi Jagdambi Temple, so called after the image of Parvati which is now enshrined in the sanctum. The original image was of Vishnu, but the replacement also dates back to the same period as the temple.

itinerary to follow the trail that his *palki* (palanquin) bearer spoke of. He recorded that he had found what was "probably the finest aggregate number of temples congregated in one place to be met in all of India, and are all within a stone's throw of one another." He copied Dhanga's stone inscription, dated AD 1002, which was lying loose in the Visvanatha temple. Although he wrote, "some of the sculptures were extremely indecent and offensive; which I was at first much surprised to find in temples," his work opened Khajuraho to future generations. Years later, Cunningham visited the site and in his 1864 report, counted 872 statues, of which 646 were on the outside walls. He studied other inscriptions, temples, loose images and ruined shrines which had turned into mounds and were scattered through the site, and was struck by the "richness of the carving" and the "profusion of sculptures."

The Temples: Microcosms of Man

When Alexander of Macedonia crossed the Indus in 326 BC, Hinduism was abstract, a philosophy, rather than ritualistic and temple worship did not exist in India. The earliest shrines which rose were simple platforms, with or without roofs. The foundations for the Hindu temple were laid during the Gupta period (3rd-5th century) when its basic characteristic elements— consisting of a square sanctum and a pillared porch—emerged. The square form of the temple was inherited through the centuries as a symbol within which energy is born. The earlier examples were made of stone and were distinguished by a flat slab roof, usually monolithic, while the later temples, built of brick or stone, developed a spire (*shikhara*). The oldest Gupta temple, at Sanchi in Madhya Pradesh, dates to the fifth century ; it has a single-cell sanctum and a portico which rested on four pillars. Evolved Gupta temples also had a covered processional path for circumambulation. Later, an ambulatory was added around the sanctum and the pillared porch gradually developed to assume the form of a hall which was often preceded by an entrance porch. A vestibule was added between the sanctum and the hall which developed lateral transepts for ventilation. During the seventh century, the sanctum was roofed by a tall curvilinear spire; this, the *shikhara*, came to characterise the most conspicuous feature of the northern temple. The spire was initially three vertical projections, then five and occasionally seven. After the seventh century, the northern temples evolved in largely regional patterns, influenced by the dynasties who patronised them.

The ornamental ceiling of the entrance porch of the Lakshmana temple is boldly carved with deep designs of floral cusps with decorative details. The bracket figures in the ceiling corners are of *apsaras*.

An image of Adinatha, the first Jain *tirthankara*, from the Shantinatha temple.

The *Shilpashastras* (art-treatises) laid down the rules for temple building in medieval India. They drew out the essential parts of a temple, the meaning and position of sculptures inside and outside temples and auspicious motifs ("birds of good augury, figures, crosses, jars, couples, foliage, tendrils and goblins"). The temple became a microcosm, a symbol of the Absolute Being, akin to the human body which is animated by the *atman*; likewise, the temple is also made of several interrelated parts, all of which form a cohesive whole. Names of parts of the body came to be used figuratively to symbolise the organic unity of the temple. The basement on which the temple is erected (*adisthana*) represents the legs; this stands on a solid block of masonry, the *jagati*. The *jangha*, the walls resting on the *jagati*, are seen as the waist, and the *shikhara* (the tower built over the sanctum) is the head. The most sacred part of the temple is the *garbhagriha* (literally womb-chamber) which contains the

main idol. A single room directly below the *shikara*, it has high walls and a dark, silent interior which only the temple priest is allowed to enter. The *garbhagriha* is joined to a hall for worshippers (*mandapa*) by a vestibule (*antarala*). The *mandapa* is approached through a portico (*ardha-mandapa*).

The prototype of the Khajuraho temple contains a *garbhagriha*, a *mandapa*, an *ardha-mandapa* and an *antarala*. Each part has its own pyramidal roof, but is not structurally separate; the smaller towers—beginning from the lowest over the porch—rise progressively to lead the eye up to the highest, the *shikhara*. The peaks are arrayed along an east-west axial line. The silhouette is of a mountain range, of graded peaks rising in a regulated crescendo. The central *shikhara* is often likened to the mythical Mount Meru, Brahma's heaven, or Mount Kailash, the mythical Himalayan abode of Lord Shiva. The Khajuraho *shikhara*, like those of most northern temples,

The Kandariya Mahadeva is the most spectacular monument of Khajuraho and marks the climax of the Khajuraho temples in terms of scale, composition and sculptural ornamentaion.

is curved for its whole length. It is often made up of miniature *shikharas* emerging from the central tower, intensifying its upward thrust, symbolic of the ascent to the highest level, heaven. A series of small *amalakas* (circular, ribbed discs) demarcate the division of each spire into storeys, breaking its vertical movement and leading each time to a peak of its own from where it starts a renewed ascent; the effect of the whole is of natural growth, suggesting that the Absolute is found in this world as well as the next. Each spire ends in a constriction which is surmounted with a large disc on which is placed the *kalash* or pot which symbolises the nectar of immortality.

The temples are built on a high plinth with an ambulatory path around the base. In the larger temples at Khajuraho — the Kandariya Mahadeva, Lakshmana and Visvanatha — a circumambulatory (*pradakshina*) around the sanctum is added, and the *mandapa* branches

out into four projections with windows for light and ventilation, giving the temple a ground plan of a duplicate cross. Temples which do not have an inner ambulatory show only one cross. The sanctum is segmented; it is *saptaratha* (seven projections in plan and elevation). The cubical section below the *shikhara* is also divided into seven carved horizontal bands (*sapta-bada*) which are separated by decorative patterns. The numerous sculptures, worked into projections and indentations, absorb the light into the texture of the walls, and the contrast of light and shadow make for an effect which is three-dimensional.

Following pages 40-41: A view of the western group of temples as seen from the Kandariya Mahadeva temple The Devi Jagdambi and the Kandariya Mahadeva are adjacent with the small, pavilion-like Mahadeva shrine between them. The man seen at the edge of the platform grappling with a lion (a symbol of the Chandella dynasty), is a recurrent theme at Khajuraho.

Sculptures: Erotic and Religious

The mass of these stone edifices, countered by intricate carvings, would appear lavish but the sculptures were alternated with linear patterns etched in deep hollows between them which allowed space. Kaimur sandstone, which was largely used in the Khajuraho temples, was most receptive to chiselling and allowed the sculptors to carve minute details like folds of garments, ornaments, drops of water, strands of hair, nails and creases of the skin. The Hindu ideal of beauty is formalised, and images made for worship were in accordance with the canons laid down in the *Shilpashatras*: the face is required to be "rounded like a hen's egg", the forehead is compared to a bow, the eyes are usually long and tapering, shaped like a fish, the eyebrows are likened to the leaves of a neem tree, the chin to a mango stone, the hands and feet to lotus flowers, the waist is slender like a wasp's, while the breasts and hips surge to roundness.

The Khajuraho builders employed corbelling, projecting horizontal blocks of stone to support vertical structures, which produced roofs like levelled domes; cement and mortar were rarely used. Sculptures were contiguous with architecture. Each slab of stone or granite was chosen, sanctified and carved before it was placed in its allotted space and any stone which got damaged would be discarded as it was considered inauspicious. The Khajuraho builders worked in an inspired flood of creativity and the sculptures, which conform to the classical traditions, are among the masterpieces of medieval India.

The sculptures have been classified broadly into five categories:

The temples of Khajuraho are known for their erotic sculptures but these are only a small part of the carvings. This panel, from the Kandariya Mahadeva temple, depicts *apsaras* in a variety of postures.

(1) Images of gods and goddesses of which the main image is placed in the sanctum. Some cult-images are worked into the broad bands which run around the external walls of the temples. Representations of spouses of the deities, demi-gods, *dikpalas*, *vidyadharas*, *gandharvas*, *kumaras* (four-armed load-bearing dwarfs, referred to in the *Mahabharata*) and *ganas*, along with the cult images, create a semblance of heaven.

(2) Panels depicting scenes from courtly life, battles, hunting scenes, processions, rituals, ceremonies and domestic life.

(3) Animals and mythical beasts, interspersed with figurative forms on the bands which girdle the temple walls. Elephants, which comprised the mainstay of medieval Indian armies, are the main subjects and have received a warm and humorous treatment. Horses, monkeys, parrots, a few camels and a lion grappling with a warrior are also depicted. The *shardula*, a mythical beast which signifies the struggle between ignorance and knowledge, is the subject of several sculptures. A combination of two animals, the lower half is usually of a horse while the upper half could be of a rampant horned lion, an elephant, a boar, camel or even a parrot. An armed human rider, signifying knowledge, is usually shown on the back of the *shardula* who attempts to devour him; he is countered by a figure representing ignorance, under the creature's feet.

(4) Geometric and floral motifs on walls, pillars and ceilings inside temples, significant as symbols or simply as visual forms.

(5) Loving couples and female figures including *surasundaris* and *apsaras* who are in attendance to deities. Some of the finest sculptures are of *apsaras*, usually located within the *mandapa* or the circumambulatory passages; they are depicted carrying water-jars, lotus-flowers and ornaments, which they offer to the gods. *Surasundaris*, often portrayed as idealised womanhood, are depicted in various moods or engaging in day-to-day human activities. They appear on the interiors of brackets and niches, in the *mandapa*, the circumambulatory and around the exterior bands of the temples and are depicted dancing, playing the flute or the vina, emerging from the bath, squeezing water from the hair, applying collyrium in the eyes and paint on the feet. The figures are often shown in a pose called *tribhanga* in which one leg is bent and the body is turned slightly at the hips, giving the effect of balance between poise and active energy. The sensuousness of the figures is accentuated by the limbs which are elongated.

Since the middle of the 19th century when Khajuraho was first documented by the British, many theories were put forward to account for the seeming incongruity of temples being adorned with erotic sculptures. Burt wrote that they were "extremely indecent and offensive" and "the most disgraceful representations to desecrate their [the Hindus'] ecclesiastic creations." Cunningham called the sculptures "disgustingly obscene." Subsequently, in the early twentieth century, art historians attempted to explain their profusion and interpret them.

Historically, *maithuna* sculptures have been depicted in India for nearly 2,000 years, possibly a consequence of the existence of fertility cults. Couples performing the sexual act have been depicted in terracotta and the sculpture of the Sunga period (2nd-1st century BC dynasty of central and eastern India) and the subsequent Amravati and Mathura schools. Cosmic creation thought of in terms of sexual union is an idea as old as the Rig Veda (believed to have been composed between 1,500 and 1,000 BC).

The Upanishads, first articulated 2,500 years

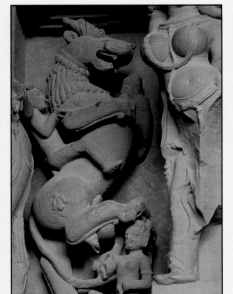

Top left: This south-facing niche from the Chitragupta temple depicts Brahma, the Hindu Creator, with his consort Saraswati, Chitragupta temple;

Right: Panel depicting a couple in embrace from Lakshmana temple, north vestibule;

Middle: The traditional horse-lion *shardula* is symbolic, representing the victory of knowledge over ignorance.

Bottom left: As entertainers of the divinities, *apsaras* with sinuous grace appear in hundreds of forms and positions mostly around the exteriors of the temples.

Right: The recessive in the pillars, ceilings and walls of the temples are carved with geometric motifs.

A *maithuna*, at best an invented posture but testimony to the sculptor's artistry, from the north band, Vishvanatha Temple.

ago, put forth the ultimate goal of man as *moksha* (salvation), the union of the human soul and the Divine Soul, merging the *atman* (individual soul) with the *Paramatman* (the Universal). Vedantic monoism gave way to *Sankhya* (literally the count), a pre-Aryan philosophical system which viewed the world as essentially dualistic, consisting of Prakriti (matter), the fountainhead of thought, substance and sensory perceptions, and Purusha (spirit) which stood apart in much the same way as the *atman* does from the body it animates. Purusha (literally man) was masculine and the passive spectator of the eternal unfolding of Prakriti which was feminine. Dissolving duality, merging Prakriti and Purusha was represented by the sexual union of man and woman which became symbolic of *moksha*.

Tantra later personified Prakriti as the wife of Purusha. Tantrism (named after the sect's scriptures, Tantra) was possibly a reactionary swing from the austere ideals of Buddhism and became a powerful religious movement which affected both Hinduism and Buddhism from the eighth to fourteenth centuries. While conventional Hinduism emphasized the renunciation of physical, emotional and tactile pleasures, Tantrism propagated the controlled enjoyment of the senses, which was likened to walking on the blade of a sword. Sex was given a ritual symbolism and even became a religious rite. After regular evening worship, Tantric rites involved indulging in the five 'm's (or *pancha makara*): *madya* (alcohol), *mamsa* (meat), *matysa* (fish), *mudra* (symbolic hand gestures) and *maithuna* (the sexual act). The *sadhaka* (worshipper) meditated on these elements to obliterate the difference between the worshipper and the worshipped and attain *samadhi* (transcendental experience). These were, however, done under strict control, for

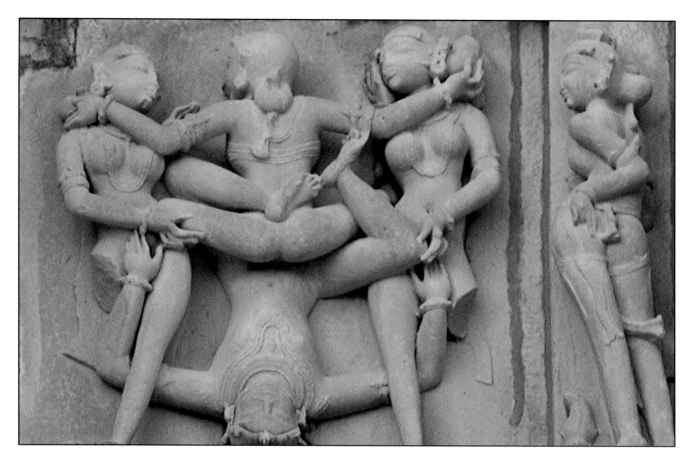

A *maithuna*, based on a yogic posture, from the south vestibule, Kandariya Mahadeva temple.

what was considered profane for the novice was sacred for initiates.

Tantric beliefs also led to the development of Shakti cults, whose followers, the Saktas, worship Shakti, a form of the Mother Goddess who is referred to in the Puranas. The Mother Goddess—whose chief form is of Shiva's consort, Parvati—is worshipped throughout India by several names, both in her benevolent and malevolent forms. Shakti, believed to be the source of creation, is believed to activate the dormant generative powers of Shiva. With her stimulus the world was created and Shiva and Shakti became manifest in nature. This aspect of Shiva, as creator of the universe, is represented by the physical union of man and woman, the individual counterpart of cosmic creation.

Hindu literature, both religious and secular, are full of sexual allusions and uninhibited erotic passages. Kama (desire and fulfilment)

was deemed to be one of the aims of life in the Smritis (sacred Hindu texts of which the Epics and Puranas are a part); its pursuit constituted a legitimate activity in the scheme of things and was a stepping stone to salvation. Some believed that the contortionist positions on the temple walls were a graphic illustration of the Kamasutra, the sage Vatsyayana's fourth-century treatise on love. The depiction of loving birds, animals and human couples was also considered auspicious for the builder and, by association, for the supplicant. Another theory is that erotic sculptures on temple walls were meant to test whether the devotee had purged his mind of worldly thoughts before he entered the temple. Other medieval Indian sects believed that *bhoga* (sensual pleasure) was an alternative path to yoga (meditation) for salvation, and sex was given a ceremonial significance.

Sacred art does not dwell on the transient, but grasps the essential. The Khajuraho temples are an enduring legacy which reflect an integrated view of life, and joy in the world as it was perceived. Life, which is sacramental to Hindus, is portrayed not for its own sake but as an aspect of the Divine; the temples, whatever the context in which they were built, depict sensual and spiritual bliss in a humanised art-form—symbols, forms and images whose organic vitality, movement and expressiveness are enhanced, effectively transcending the mundane for the sublime.

Top: A frieze from the Lakshmana temple.
Left: This *maithuna* is from a small niche facing north in a lower band of the Vishvanatha temple.
Facing page: Some of the most proportionate sculptures are from the Vishvanatha temple. These are from its north-facing middle and upper bands.

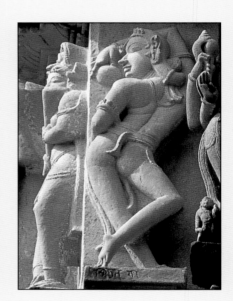

Apsaras and *surasundaris*, represented as youthful, voluptuous women with winsome charm, are an integral part of the sculptural content of the temples. They are shown in a variety of alluring poses, portraying different moods. *Apsaras* removing a thorn from the foot, applying vermilion on the forehead, singing, dancing, playing the flute, painting the foot and applying collyrium appear in the interiors of brackets, niches, in the circumambulatory and on the facades of the temples.

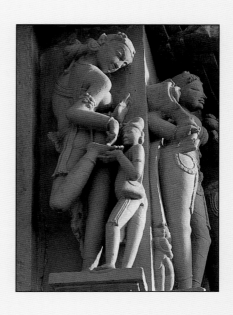

Guide to the Temples

The temples are classified into three broad groups: western, eastern and southern.

WESTERN GROUP

The western group, set in a beautiful park, is situated to the north of the Shiv Sagar tank. This closely packed group is believed to cover what was originally a sacred lake, and contains almost all the larger temples of Khajuraho, with the exception of Parsvanatha and Duladeo. Two of these, the Lakshmana and the Vishvanatha, are specifically recorded to have been built by kings, while a third, Kandariya Mahadeva which is the most spectacular temple of Khajuraho, was obviously a royal construction. The larger temples of this group face east and run north-south in two parallel rows on opposite sides of the park. All the temples of this group are Shiva or Vaishnava, except the Chitragupta temple which is the only Sun temple at Khajuraho.

Chausath Yogini Temple (late 9th century): On a low granite outcrop, about 400 m to the south of the Kandariya Mahadeva, stands the Chausath Yogini temple, now mostly in ruins. This is the earliest temple of Khajuraho and is simple in its plan and design, with hardly any carvings. Unlike

The interior and exterior walls of the Kandariya Mahadeva temple are profusely carved.

most of the later temples which are made of sandstone, the Chausath Yogini temple is made entirely of granite. A small ruined shrine of Ganesha, enshrining an image of the deity which is now in the local museum, stood in front of the temple.

This temple is raised upon a high platform and consists of a rectangle of crudely constructed small square shrines each of which has a pyramidal roof. Of the original sixty-four (*chausath*) shrines dedicated to the yoginis (attendants of Kali, a malevolent form of the Mother Goddess), thirty-five still stand; three yogini images are enshrined in the shrine in the centre of the rear wall facing the entrance.

Lalguan Mahadeva Temple (*c.* AD 900): The Lalguan Mahadeva temple stands on a granite outcrop, about 600m to the west of the Chausath Yogini temple is. Built of granite and sandstone, this shrine, now in ruins, was constructed on the eastern bank of Lalguan Sagar, the western limit of the old town. It is simple in plan and design, and has no carved decorations. It belongs to the

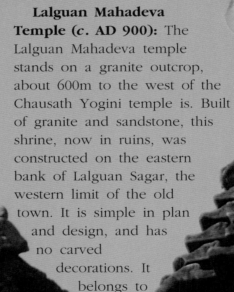

period of transition from granite to sandstone; it stands on a high granite *jagati*, while sandstone was introduced for the *shikhara*, only parts of which still stand.

Varaha Temple (*c*. AD 900-925): Close to the north bank of the Shiv Sagar, facing the Lakshmana temple lies the Varaha temple. Its small rectangular pavilion is elevated on a terrace and has a stepped pyramidal roof. Within the sanctuary is a highly polished yellow sandstone image of Varaha, Lord Vishnu's third incarnation in which he took the form of a boar to save the world. The image of Varaha is covered with 674 figures of gods and goddesses. Between the feet of Varaha and the pedestal is a figure of the serpent Seshanaga (the serpent of eternity) whose tail, described by Cunningham, is now broken. Also underneath it are the feet of a broken figure of the earth goddess Bhu-devi. The elaborately detailed lotus ceiling, with three concentric rows of petals, is carved in full relief and is one of the finest at Khajuraho.

Matangeshvara Temple (*c*. AD 900-925): The Matangeshvara temple is adjacent to the Lakshmana temple. It stands on a high platform and is approached by steps on its east. A flag on its simple pyramid-shaped roof proclaims it is still in use for worship; the roof is crowned by several successive *amalakas*.

Deep balconies with overhanging eaves project from three sides of its sanctuary walls; on its east is the entrance porch. Enshrined within the sanctuary, with several inscriptions on its surface, is a large polished sandstone Shiva linga, Lord Shiva's attribute which characterises him as the god of fertility.

Lakshmana Temple (*c*. AD 930-950): The Lakshmana temple stands in the heart of a large cluster of temples near Shiv Sagar. This temple is the earliest and best preserved of the mature Chandella temples. It is dedicated to the triple-headed four-armed Vaikuntha form of Vishnu. The temple is attributed to King Yasovarman. An inscribed slab which was originally excavated at the base of the temple is now fixed in the passageway around the sanctum.

The main temple is built on a high platform terrace and is surrounded by four subsidiary shrines. Although the Kandariya Mahadeva and Vishvanatha temples are also of the *panchayatana* (five-shrined) type, only the Lakshmana temple preserves all four corner shrines. The subsidiary shrines, which have only a single curvilinear shaft, are smaller and simpler than the principal temple, but they also incorporate carved panels and ornamented doorways.

The entrance is by imposing steps which run up the middle of the east side. Friezes on the terrace basement depict processions of horses, elephants, camels, battle scenes, dancers and musicians, domestic and erotic scenes, deities, ascetics with women, and ritualised sexual acts. Beautifully carved elephants at the base are built as if they were supporting the temple. The temple also has one of the finest specimens of apsara brackets.

The temple is entered through an elegant two-looped *makara-torana* (arch with carved crocodiles) flanked by gladiators. A pillared hall, at the corner of which are carved brackets with *apsaras*, leads to the sanctum. Eight figures on each column represent the eight sects of Tantra.

The doorway of the sanctum are adorned with carvings and bands which depict lions, Vishnu incarnations (as a fish, tortoise, boar and his composite form with a central human head flanked by boar and lion heads) and the *Navagrahas* (nine planetary deities including Chandra, Surya, Mangala and Rahu). The sanctum is *panch-ratha* (five projections) and enshrines an image of Vishnu as Vaikuntha. Two bands of carved panels, depicting *apsaras* and *surasundaris* in the projections and

Facing page: The sanctum floor of the Matangeshvara temple is largely covered by an enormous polished *linga*.

Following pages 56-57: Two bands of sculpture from the Lakshmana temple. The top band has a divine couple flanked by female musicians. On either side are four-armed images of Vishnu, the Hindu Preserver.

The passage around the sanctum of the Lakshmana temple has several exquisite sculptures. On the right is Gajalakshmi, Vishnu's consort. The figure with the beard is Agni, the god of fire. Interspersed are images of celestial nymphs.

couples in complicated sexual acts in the recesses cover the exterior walls of the passageway below the main tower. The *apsaras* and *surasundaris* are in attendance to the deities, bearing offerings, dancing or playing musical instruments, dressing or wringing out their wet hair. The additional porches are separated by balconies and angled eaves.

The best examples of medieval art adorn the *jangha* (walls); those of a pair of minstrels, their faces expressing devotional rapture, and a dancing Ganesha on the southern facade are among the finest.

Vishvanatha Temple (AD 1002): The Vishvanatha temple is built near a ruined tank called Dhugavan. This temple is dedicated to Shiva in his aspect as Lord of the Universe. According to an inscribed slab now in the temple porch, this temple was built by King Dhangadeva. It anticipates the Kandariya Mahadeva which marks the culmination of the

Chandella style, but is laid out in much the same manner as the Lakshmana temple which predates it, introducing subtle variations in the main shrine—the basement has smaller niches, doubled in two tiers. Only two out of four subsidiary shrines are intact.

The outer facade has the traditional three broad bands of sculpture. The high basement on the terrace has fine scrollwork, carvings of processions of men and animals, and amorous couples. The basement niches are carved with the *Saptamatrikas* (Seven Mothers) with Ganesha and Virabhadra.

A richly adorned doorway provides access to the sanctuary which originally had an emerald *linga* in addition to the present one enshrined in the sanctuary.

Within the temple, the main hall and passageway around the shrine contain some of the loveliest sculptures, including one of a woman with a fruit in one hand and a parrot in the

A *maithuna* from the north-facing middle band of the Vishvanatha temple.

other, a mother with her child, amorous couples, a *surasundari* playing the flute and another, notable for her charming expression, painting her foot. The ceiling has elaborate patterns of many-petalled flowers and hanging stamens.

East of the temple, sharing its raised platform, is an open pavilion housing a large Nandi image; the basement has a frieze of elephants. The pavilion has a pyramidal roof of horizontal elements.

Parvati Temple (AD 950-1000): The Parvati temple, a heavily-restored small temple located southwest of Vishvanatha temple, originally comprised a sanctum and a porch. The porch is completely lost, but the platform survives and the carved doorway retains some of its original decoration. The image inside the sanctum is of Gauri, an aspect of Parvati, with the *godha* (iguana) as her vehicle.

Devi Jagadambi Temple (early 11th century): The Devi Jagadambi temple shares a platform with the Kandariya Mahadeva temple.

Originally dedicated to Vishnu, the image within the sanctum is one of Parvati as goddess of the world; this is not the original image but dates to the same period as the temple. The temple follows the same scheme as the Chitragupta temple but its hall has a square ceiling, an increased emphasis on the *mandapa* and its massive pyramidal roof. The carvings on the outer walls are among the best; they include several of Vishnu, one of Yama (the god of death), amorous couples and *surasundaris* whose sinuous postures and expressions of intense absorption characterise them as masterpieces of the fully developed Chandella style.

Chitragupta Temple (early 11th century): Chitragupta temple is the only Khajuraho temple dedicated to Surya, and demonstrates an evolution when compared with the Lakshamana and Vishvanatha monuments. It closely resembles the Devi Jagadambi which predates it. The Chitragupta temple comprises

Top: The back wall of the Devi Jagdambi temple has the deities of the Hindu trinity in their various incarnations. The figure in the lower panel is that of Vamana, the dwarf incarnation of Vishnu; the central panel depicts Shiva as Mrityunjaya (one who has conquered death); the upper panel has Brahma with his consort Savitri.
Left: This damaged image of lovers is from the lower, south-west facing band of Chitragupta temple.

a sanctum without an ambulatory, a vestibule, a hall with lateral transepts and an entrance porch. The ceiling of the hall has developed from a simple square of the early Chandella temples to an elaborate octagon. The outer walls of the passageway have small niches carved with some of the finest figures of *surasundaris*, *dikpalas*, erotic couples and deities, including an eleven-headed Vishnu which signifies his ten incarnations, in the central niche of the southern facade. Three tiers of panels depict processions of stone-carriers, hunting scenes and elephant fights. The sanctuary has a fine carved doorway and enshrines an image of Surya, riding a chariot of seven horses.

Clockwise from top: A panel from the east-facing wall close to the entrance portico of the Devi Jagdambi temple; fluid body movements combined with self-contained expressions give the Khajuraho sculptures much of their sensuousness; each sculpture has its mood and character and stands both alone and as part of a frieze.

Shiva Temple (11th century): The Shiva temple, a ruined monument, stands on the terrace that links the Devi Jagadambi and Kandariya Mahadeva temples. Only an isolated sanctuary doorway sheltered by a porch survives; within the porch is a *shardula* and a crouching female figure.

Kandariya Mahadeva Temple (c. 1025-50): Kandariya Mahadeva temple, dedicated to Shiva, is Khajuraho's most magnificent temple and marks the climax of the series in terms of scale, composition and sculptural ornamentation. The schemes of the Lakshmana and Vishvanatha temples are developed here. The platform is three metres high, and the *shikhara*, rising to a height of 31m, is almost as

The *makara torana* is an ornamental gateway made of a single stone, carved into four loops, culminating in crocodile heads. This style of *makara torana* survives only in three temples: Lakshmana, Kandariya Mahadeva and Javari.

long as it is high. Eighty-four smaller projections are carried upwards to the *shikhara* in a great sweep resulting in a superstructure which is visually somewhat restless but unified. The graded hall roofs and *shikhara* signify the mythical Mount Kailash in the Himalayas.

The temple is approached by a flight of stairs. Over the entrance to the porch is a four-looped *makara torana* carved from a single stone. An elaborately carved doorway with mythical animals, *apsaras* and the river goddesses Ganga and Yamuna, leads to the sanctuary where a marble *linga* is installed. Niches in the sanctuary walls house images of Shiva.

Eight hundred sculptures are carved on its interior and exterior walls. Three bands of sculpture on the outer walls depict gods and goddesses including aspects of Shiva, *dikpalas*, *maithunas* and *surasundaris* in the projections interspersed with mythical beasts in the

reccesses. *Apsaras* in a variety of alluring positions are particularly notable for their slender form. The erotic sculptures are concentrated on the northern and southern facade, in the juncture between the shrine and the main hall. The roof of the *mandapa* is also intricately carved and the basement is provided with processional friezes that illustrate courtly themes, warriors and hunters, acrobats, musicians, dancers, devotees and amorous couples. Niches in the basement house figures of goddesses carved almost all around.

EASTERN GROUP

Brahma Temple (*c.* AD 900): Brahma temple stands on a bank of the Khajurasagar. This simple square structure consists of a sanctum

Facing page: Panels from the Kandariya Mahadeva Temple.

This panel from the Adinatha temple depicts a luminary being attended to while visitors pay their respects.

and a porch. It was wrongly attributed to Brahma because of a four-faced *linga* now enshrined in the sanctum, but it is really a Vaishnava temple. A figure of Vishnu is carved on the lintel of the sanctum doorway. The temple, which belongs to the early structural phase of Lalguan Mahadeva, has a body made of granite while the *shikhara* is made of sandstone. Its pyramidal roof is divided into several horizontal mouldings. The temple is much restored.

Vamana Temple (*c.* AD 1050-75): The Vamana temple is dedicated to Vishnu who in his fifth incarnation is said to have taken the form of a dwarf (Vamana) and tricked the demon Bali into granting him as much land as he could cover in three strides. The dwarf became a giant, strode the universe in three

Facing page: A panel from the Parsvanatha temple. Vishnu, with his characteristic attributes, the wheel and conch-shell, is depicted with his consort Lakshmi.

strides and staked his claim from Bali, thus depriving the latter of his domain. The temple, which is an example of the fully evolved Chandella style, has a *shikhara* without clustered elements and no ambulatory. The *shikhara* rises in bands that continue the projections of the walls beneath. These bands are covered with a grid of arch-like patterns; the summit is surmounted by an *amalaka* and pot-finial. The outer walls have only two bands of sculptures which include sensuous *surasundaris*, many of which are damaged, but erotic sculptures do not feature here. Within, in the main niches of the sanctum, are figures of the Divine Trinity (Brahma, Vishnu and Shiva). A richly carved doorway leads to the sanctum which houses an image of the four-armed Vamana.

Javari Temple (*c.* AD 1075-1100): The Javari temple, a small temple, is notable for its soaring slender *shikhara*. It is raised on a plain terrace, with three bands of richly carved

sculptures on the outer walls. A particularly fine *makara-torana* is preserved over the entrance.

Parsvanatha Temple (mid-10th century): The Parsvanatha temple is the largest and finest Jain temple of the Chandella period. It was originally dedicated to the first *tirthankara* Adinatha—the Jaina figures on the lintel indicate the dedication—but a black image of Parsvanatha was placed in the sanctum in 1860. The temple is dominated by a curvilinear tower with numerous clustered elements similar to the Lakshmana temple. The outer walls are solid with three bands of sculptures. There are no balconies but light enters through fretted windows. On the walls are numerous Vaishnava images including Parasurama, Balarama and Revati, a group of Rama, Sita and Hanuman and episodes from the Krishna legend. The temple also has some of the most beautiful figures of *surasundaris* in different postures: notable among these are those of one applying collyrium, of one painting her feet (seen on the southern facade), and of another putting on anklets (on the northern facade). Within the shrine are figures of *tirthankaras* which are rather rigid and in contrast to the sculptures on the outer walls.

The interior doorway is richly carved. The jambs are adorned with river goddesses (believed to wash away sins), attendants and guardian figures.

Ghantai Temple (late 10th century): Ghantai Temple gets its name from the fine bell (*ghantai*) motifs carved on its elegant pillars. It was essentially of the same design as the Parsvanatha temple, but nearly twice its size. Little survives of the temple besides an entrance porch, a hall supported by four pillars and a richly ornamented doorway. The ceiling of the entrance porch is exquisitely carved with groups of dancers and singers.

Adinatha Temple (late 11th century): The Adinatha Temple lies immediately to the north of the Parsavanatha temple. It has a single shaft for the tower which is covered with a mesh of arch-like motifs. Only the sanctum

These panels from the south-west wall of the Duladeo temple are of Shiva depicted with his consort Parvati. The figure on the left in the upper panel is that of Nandi, Shiva's mount. Yama, the god of death, is positioned just below.

and vestibule have survived; the attached porch is a later addition. The three bands of wall sculptures depict *surasundaris* and flying *vidyadharas*. The niches have *yakshis*, and the corners have *dikpalas*.

SOUTHERN GROUP

This comprises two standing temples, Chaturbhuj and Deoladeo.

Chaturbhuj Temple (*c.* AD 1100): Chaturbhuj Temple lies three kilometres south of the village, a little south of Khudar Nala

Facing page: The Adinatha temple is girdled by three bands of elegant sculptures including surasundaris and flying vidyadharas.
Following pages 68-69: Sculptures on the south facade, Parsvanatha temple.

Columns from the Duladeo temple. Flying *vidyadharas* in the top row seem poised in movement.

which flows through the southern portion of the town and once formed an important feature of the ancient town. It anticipates the Deoladeo temple, but was built when sculptural art was on the decline. Although the temple is girdled by the usual three bands of sculptures, the figures are stereotyped and expressionless. The sanctum, however, houses the largest image of Shiva in Khajuraho (some scholars think it might be of Vishnu).

Duladeo Temple (c. AD 1100-50): The Duladeo (meaning holy bridegroom, a reference to Shiva) temple, standing south of the Ghantai temple, was built on the north bank of the Khudar Nala. This is one of the last temples of the Chandella era and exhibits the exhaustion of the vitality for which the Khajuraho temples are famous. The sculptures are lavishly ornamented but lack depth and become repetitive. It has a large number of Shiva sculptures, perhaps more than any other temple.

ARCHAEOLOGICAL MUSEUM

The museum lies near the entrance to the Western group of temples, and contains near 2,000 10th-11th century sculptures retrieved over fifty years from the site.

The entrance to the museum is a temple doorway. Among the finest exhibits are a large dancing Ganesha figure (*c.* AD 1130) which stands in the entrance hall, a panel depicting two *tirthankaras* (*c.* AD 1635) and a standing Surya figure surrounded by miniature attendants (*c.* AD 1262). In the Vaishnava gallery are numerous sculptures of the various incarnations of Vishnu; among them is one of Varaha (*c.* AD 861). Seated images of Buddha (*c.* AD 450) and a five-headed Shiva (*c.* AD 1098) are also displayed.

Facing page: Tourists looking at a panel on the facade of the Devi Jagdambi temple.

70

Cult images were distinguished by their attributes, headdress or mounts. Mildly erotic representations of deities with their consorts created an aspect of heaven. Sculptures of Vishnu-Lakshmi and Revati-Balram hint at compassion and spirituality, while that of lovers with oversized noses has a humorous note.

The *maithuna* in Khajuraho is possibly a historical growth of the simple *maithuna* occurring in early Indian art. Portrayals of expressions of sexual arousal had a religious sanction and the union of man and woman in which duality is lost came to symbolise *moksha* (liberation).

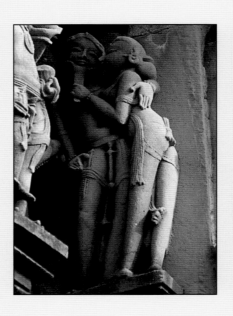

Orchha

Orchha, 170 kilometres from Khajuraho, was built during the 16th and 17th centuries by the Bundela rulers of the area. Largely untouched by the present, the picturesque city of Orchha retains much of its medieval character and remains as if in a time warp.

The Bundela Rajput chieftain, Raja Rudra Pratap (1501-31), chose this site as his capital as it was situated on an island of rock along a bend in the Betwa river and elevated above the surrounding area. He built a wall around an existing settlement; the fort occupied most of the island. His successor, Raja Bharti Chand, completed the city walls and citadel and built the first of three palaces. These were set in an open quadrangle, with a multi-arched bridge spanning them. Subsequent rulers added to Orchha, until it became a prosperous city.

The prosperity of Orchha was enhanced by the Bundelas' favourable links with the Mughals. Though the Bundela ruler, Madhukar Shah, was defeated in battle by Akbar, the Mughal emperor, he managed to win the latter's friendship. His successor, Bir Singh Deo (1605-26), affiliated himself with Akbar's son, Prince Salim (later Jahangir). At the latter's instigation, Bir Singh Deo had Abul Fazl (Akbar's trusted prime minister and author of the *Akbar Nama*) murdered in cold blood when he was returning from the south with a caravan of treasure. With the reward Bir Singh Deo received for this act, he financed the construction of Orchha.

Facing page: Pilgrims camping on the banks of the river Betwa in Orchha. The perfect medieval city, it is now little more than a village, miles from the nearest city.
Following pages 76-77: Lakshminarayana temple (illuminated) and the silhouetted spires of the Ram Raja temple. One of the most unusual temples in India, the Ram Raja temple, originally a palace, is linked by a flag-stone path to the Lakshminarayana temple.

Bir Singh's son, Jhujan Singh, was one of the premier nobles at Jahangir's court, and enjoyed complete autonomy in the administration of Orchha. However, Jhujan Singh fell out with Jahangir's son, Shah Jahan, when he killed the chief of neighbouring Chauragarh against the wishes of the Mughals. Orchha was plundered by the Mughals in retaliation. In 1783, Orchha was finally deserted when the Bundela capital shifted to Tikamgarh.

The **Ramji Mandir**, the first of the three palaces, is the prototype of Bundela Rajput architecture. It has a central rectangular courtyard around which apartments rise on receding platforms. The outer walls glitter with blue tiles.

The second palace, the **Raj Mandir**, was built between 1554 and 1591 by the deeply religious Madhukar Shah. Its plain exterior, a solid single block crowned by *chhatris* (umbrella-like memorial cenotaphs), gives way to the royal chambers in which exquisite murals from Hindu mythology line the walls and ceilings.

The third and the most imposing of the three palaces is the **Jahangir Mahal**, built by Raja Bir Singh Ji Deo to commemorate the visit of the Mughal emperor to Orchha. The 70 m square palace has a smaller interior courtyard with a central fountain around which are apartments and terraces in three storeys. Each corner bastion is capped by a dome. Hanging balconies with wide eaves run along the exterior walls and are counterbalanced by delicate *chhatris* and trellis work, making for an effect of extraordinary richness. Windows and terraces overlook the Betwa river on the banks of which are the memorial cenotaphs of the Orchha kings. About half of the fifteen royal *chhatris*, grouped on the Kanchana ghat of the Betwa, are well preserved and appear to be etched against the evening sky, presenting

Chhatris across the river Betwa. Fifteen memorials to the rulers of Orchha are grouped along the Kanchana ghat of the river.

a particularly enchanting sight. The interiors of the palace exhibit the finest specimen of the Bundela school of painting.

Within the fort are also numerous shrines, memorials and monuments. The architecture is a hybrid of traditional Hindu and elaborate Mughal. The **Rai Praveen Mahal**, a two-storeyed brick palace, was built by Raja Indramani (who ruled between 1672-76) for a beautiful musician-courtesan of his court. The structure was designed to match the height of the trees in the surrounding landscaped garden of Anand Mahal. The **Ram Raja Temple,** also within the fort, was originally a palace but turned into a temple. Following the appearance of the god Rama in a dream, Madhukar Shah brought a statue of Rama from the venerated city of Ayodhya to his own capital, and placed it in the palace while a temple, the Chaturbhuj, was being built for it. When the idol proved impossible

to move, the pious king recalled the deity's edict in the dream that the image should remain where it was first installed. Thus, despite its soaring spires and ornate architecture, the palace became a temple and has remained so. It is also the only temple in the country where Rama is worshipped as a king rather than a deity.

The **Chaturbhuj Temple**, reached by a steep flight of steps, was built by Madhukar Shah for his queen Kunwari. Laid out in the form of a cross on a large stone platform, it has delicate exterior ornamentation with lotus emblems and religious symbols. A tall *shikhara* (spire) rises over the sanctum which is chastely plain with high walls emphasizing its sanctity.

A stone path links the Ram Raja Temple to the **Lakshminarayana Temple** which fuses elements of fort architecture in temple moulds. The interiors contain some of the

A part of Orchha's fort complex. Seen in the distance, right, is the Ram Raja temple. Approached by a multi-arched bridge, the fort complex has three palaces set in an open quadrangle.

most exquisite murals and wall paintings of the Bundela school of painting.

Also worth visiting is **Phool Bagh**, a formal garden complex, testimony to the refined aesthetic sensibilities of the Bundelas. A central row of fountains, no longer in use, culminates in an eight-pillared palace pavilion. A subterranean apartment below used to be the summer retreat of the Orchha kings. A system of water ventilation is believed to have connected the underground palace with Chandan Katora, (literally, silver bowl), a bowl-like fountain from which drops of water filtered down like raindrops.

Shahid Smarak (Martyrs' Memorial), which commemorates the freedom fighter Chandrashekhar Azad who lived in Orchha in 1926-27, now houses a library and museum. Another small palace, **Sunder Mahal**, now almost in ruins, is still a place of sanctity for Muslims. It belonged to the grandson of Bir Singh Deo, Dhurbjan, who embraced Islam after he married a Muslim girl and spent the latter part of his life in prayer. He came to be venerated as a saint and his palace became a revered site of pilgrimage.

The shrines of **Siddh Baba ka Sthan**, the **Jugal Kishore Mandir** and **Janaki Mandir** are also worth seeing. Today, Orchha is a remote village with a population of no more than a few thousand. Rarely visited, it is a haven of tranquillity and the route leading to it through forested and gently undulating countryside is very attractive. Situated on the Jhansi-Khajuraho road, it is the ideal overnight halt between Gwalior and Khajuraho (170 km), or a day-trip worth making from Datia or Jhansi.

Excursions

Though the temples of Khajuraho are a powerful lure, there are several places of interest near Khajuraho worth visiting.

AJAYGARH FORT (61 km from Khajuraho via Panna, 26 km from Kalanjar): This fort, built in the 9th century by the Chandella kings, stands at a height of 688 m on a granite outcrop. Of the five main gates only two are now accessible. An outer rampart encircles the hill and is studded with ruins of ancient Hindu sculptures and carvings which were used by the Muslims to reinforce the fortifications.

In 1809, the British Indian Army bombarded the fort after a local chief, Lakshman Daowa, defied them. The barrage remains where it fell, now encroached by teak and ebony forests.

DATIA (192 km from Khajuraho): Datia finds mention in the epic, *Mahabharata*. The seven-storey Nrising Dev Palace (Govind Mandir), the cenotaphs of the former ruling family, a temple with Mughal frescoes and the Gopeshwar temple are places of historical interest.

Nrising Dev Palace, built by Raja Bir Singh Deo (*c.* 1620), is regarded as one of the finest examples of domestic architecture. Along with the palace at Orchha, it is the best surviving specimen of 16th and 17th century architecture that developed under the Bundela Rajputs. The southern side of the palace overlooks a large lake, the Karna Sagar. Datia is worth visiting.

JHANSI (158 km from Khajuraho): Jhansi is best known for its fine fort and its legendary queen, Lakshmi Bai, a heroine of the Indian Mutiny of 1857, who died fighting the British.

The fort was built by Raja Bir Deo in 1613, with concentric walls, 5.5-9 m high and ten gates. The British breached the wall between Sainyar and Jhirna gates during the assault of 1858. The city extends beyond the old wall which has been modernised. Rani Mahal, once Lakshmi Bai's home, is now a museum. Retribution Hill, northeast of the railway station, marks the last stand of the rebels in the mutiny.

KALANJAR FORT (100 km from Khajuraho): One of the most ancient sites in Bundelkhand, Kalanjar was a venerated hill shrine (sanctified as the abode of Lord Shiva) for Hindu sadhus and pilgrims long before it was fortified and occupied by successive invaders.

The fort stands on the last spur of the Vindhya hills overlooking the Gangetic plains. It is believed to have been built during the Gupta period (AD 3rd-5th) before being captured by the Chandella ruler, Yasovarman, in the middle of the 10th century. The only approach is from the north, through seven gates, the names of which correspond to the seven stations through which the soul is believed to pass before being integrated with Brahma, the Absolute. Beyond the last gate is a drop of 3.6 m leading to Sita Sej, a stone couch set in a chamber carved from rock (4th century), and further ahead a passage leading to the Patalganga (underground river) which runs through the fort.

PANNA NATIONAL PARK (32 km from Khajuraho): Comprising 543 sq km of dense teak jungle over valleys and plateaux bordering the river Ken, Panna National Park is home to a variety of wildlife, including the tiger, panther, wolf, and also attracts a variety of birds. Paradise flycatchers, Madhya Pradesh's state bird, are found in profusion. There is also a *gharial* (crocodile) sanctuary in the vicinity of the spectacular Raneh falls.

RAJGARH (25 km north of Khajuraho): Rajgarh has a majestic 150-year old hilltop palace. The sleepy village comes to life on Tuesdays when the local people gather here for the weekly market.

SHIVPURI (293 km from Khajuraho): The former summer capital of the Scindia rulers of Gwalior, Shivpuri has exquisite palaces, intricately carved marble *chhatris* and hunting lodges. The Sakhia Sagar and Madhav Sagar lakes are surrounded by the Madhav National Park (160 sq km of deciduous forest) which is home to the tiger, leopard, deer, wild dog and sloth bear. The lakes harbour the Indian crocodile. In the nearby Karera Bird Sanctuary, one can find the Great Indian Bustard, once on the brink of extinction.